ABUNDANT TRUTH INTERNATIONAL MINISTRIES

Abundant Truth International's Devotional Series

PATHWAY TO PURPOSE (Volume III)
*
Daily Meditations for the Christian Journey

Written by: Roderick Levi Evans

Pathway to Purpose (Volume III)
Daily Meditations for the Christian Journey

All Rights Reserved ©2022 by Roderick L. Evans

No part of this book may be reproduced or transmitted in any form or by any means, graphic, electronic, or mechanical, including photocopying, recording, taping, or by any information storage or retrieval system, without the permission in writing from the publisher.

Front & Back Cover Designs by Abundant Truth Publishing

Abundant Truth Publishing
an imprint of Kingdom Builders International Ministries
For information address:
Abundant Truth International
P.O. Box 126
Camden, NC 27921

Unless otherwise indicated, all of the scripture quotations are taken from the *Authorized King James Version* **of the Bible. Scripture quotations marked with NIV are taken from the** *New International Version* **of the Bible. Scripture quotations marked with ASV are taken from the** *American Standard Version* **of the Bible. Scripture quotations marked with GW are taken from the** *God's Word Bible.*

ISBN: 978-1-60141-594-3

Printed in the United States of America.

Contents

Introduction
Day 1 – *A Reason to Love*   1

Day 2 – *Call on Him*   3

Day 3 – *Sorrowing into Salvation*   5

Day 4 – *A Protective Anger*   7

Day 5 – *Moving the Heavens*   9

Day 6 – *Angels to the Rescue*   11

Day 7 – *Victorious Voice*   13

Day 8 – *He Still Controls the Seas*   15

Day 9 – *Escaping My Enemies*   17

Day 10 – *Make Room for Me*   19

Day 11 – *Keep It Holy*   21

Day 12 – *If You Are Wondering*   23

Day 13 – *I Just Don't Know*   25

Day 14 – *The Reason for the Season*   29

Day 15 – *Blessed Assurance*   31

Day 16 – *I Can't Go Back*   33

Day 17 – *Anyway You Bless Me*   35

Day 18 – *Don't Give Up*   37

Day 19 – *All Things are Possible*   39

Day 20 – *In His Name*   41

Introduction

The Christian life is comparable to a journey. There are obstacles along the way. Rough roads and inclement weather await. However, God has given us to tools of prayer and devotion to remain fresh and vibrant during the Christian's journey with God. The Abundant Truth Devotional Series was developed to assist the Christian in personal devotion, meditation, and prayer.

The third volume of the Pathway to Purpose Devotional comprises of 30 daily devotions developed from Psalm 18 a song of David's deliverance and exaltation to the throne, along with other biblical verses. This devotional series is designed to give Christians faith and hope as they strive to fulfill their God-given purpose. In the end, the walk and life of the Christian, today, will be enhanced. Volume 3 of 3.

Day 1

A Reason to Love

David declares his Love

Have you ever truly loved something or someone? I am not talking about infatuation, but actual heartfelt emotions. Love is an emotion that demands a response or action.

When someone loves, usually they want to express their love and reasons for it; how much the more the Christian for the presence of God in their lives?

> *I will love thee, O LORD, my strength. The LORD is my rock, and my fortress, and my deliverer; my God, my strength, in whom I will trust; my buckler, and the horn of my salvation, and my high*

tower. Psalm 18:1-2 (KJV)

David, as he opened this psalm, declared his determination to love God. It was definitely not without a cause. Based upon God's wonderful works and divine intervention demonstrated in his life, David was moved to place of sheer adoration. He then lists some of God's mighty acts and attributes.

As Christians, we should not allow present distresses and frustrations to make us forgetful of God's mighty works in our lives. He not only saved us, but also continually walks with us through His presence and we see His love demonstrated as He hears our prayers.

We love Him because He first loved us. On today, reaffirm your love for Him, knowing that He will be your deliverer, strength, and fortress in present troubles. He has promised that He will never leave you nor forsake you.

Prayer of the Day:

"Lord, help me not to be forgetful to express my love to You. Though problems will arise, I welcome your peace and strength. And for that, I will love you my Lord. Amen."

Charge of the Day:

Interrupt your routine on today. Spend extra time in prayer or reading the Bible or inspirational book.

Thought of the Day:

Interruptions may change your plans, but can push you into God's plan.

Day 2

Call on Him

David calls upon the Lord

Do you know someone whom you consider dependable: an individual, in the time of trouble, who will do their best to come through for you? It is a wonderful feeling to know that they will be there for you, sometimes even when wrong choices brought the negative circumstances to you.

Every Christian must remember that they have someone to call upon when they are in distress: someone who is always there and always cares.

I will call upon the Lord, who is worthy to be praised: so shall I be saved from mine

enemies. Psalms 18:3 (KJV)

David understood this truth. No matter how many times he found himself in trouble. Regardless of the number of times his life was in danger, David endeavored to call upon the name of the Lord. However, some on today may feel as if there is no need to call upon the Lord or prayer because it seems like things are not changing or getting better.

David stated that God has earned (is worthy of) praise. If we are honest, we can think of many things that the Lord has done for us. We cannot allow present problems to deter us from trusting in Him.

In the same manner that David declared his salvation from his enemies, Christians will be delivered from those things, which challenge their faith, peace, and hope in Christ. Continue to call upon the Lord, for everyone (Jesus said) who asks receives.

Prayer of the Day:

"I thank you for your promises God. I trust that you are with me and will deliver me and answer me as you did David. I thank you now. Amen"

Charge of the Day:

Think on His promises and respond with a declaration of thanksgiving.

Thought of the Day:

A promise is like a check, it can only be cashed when you take it to bank.

Day 3

Sorrowing Into Salvation

David recalls God's Intervention

Times of sadness will come. However, the Christian can have hope regardless of the type of sadness that comes. How? It is possible through the presence of Christ. David recalled times of sadness and personal threat, but he also said that these led him to call on God's name.

> *The sorrows of death compassed me and the floods of ungodly men made me afraid. The sorrows of hell compassed me about: the snares of death prevented me. In my distress I called upon the LORD, and cried unto my God: he heard my voice out of his temple, and my cry came before*

him, even into his ears. Psalms 18:4-6 (KJV)

As Christians, we are not exempt from troubles, disappointments, grief, and sadness. Yet, we are to remember to call upon the name of the Lord through prayer. In doing so, we can receive comfort, peace, and strength. As we draw closer to Him in times of sorrow, we place ourselves in a position to experience His salvation.

He will save us from sinking into depression and into despair. He will save us from ourselves, that we should not be a burden to ourselves when sad, sorrowful, and grievous times surface. Regardless of the pain or discomfort you may face on today, trust that as you call on His name, He will give you His grace.

Prayer of the Day:

"God, give me grace and comfort as I face disappoint, despair, and sadness in this life. I trust you will never leave me nor forsake me. Amen."

Charge of the Day:

Tell someone about a time when Christ provided comfort to you.

Thought of the Day:

Life is like a day. It only comes once so you have to make the most of it.

Day 4

A Protective Anger
God protects David

To care for and protect what we love is an enduring human trait. Many of us have family members who came to our rescue when threats from others surfaced.

I know of this oh so well! My older brother would quickly come to my defense in my formative years. He did not care if I was responsible for the trouble or not, he would come to my aid.

I am not advocating, in any way, ungodly behavior and actions justified through protecting those who we love. However, we can identify somewhat with how God will protect us because of His love.

> ***Then the earth shook and trembled; the foundations also of the hills moved and were shaken, because he was wroth. There went up a smoke out of his nostrils, and fire out of his mouth devoured: coals were kindled by it. Psalms 18:7-8 (KJV)***

Continuing our examination of Psalm 18, we discover that God's protective love surfaced when David was in trouble. From David's metaphoric description, we see how God will move heaven and earth on our behalf because of His love.

Today, you can trust that God will be there for you. He declared that He was a jealous God and would not leave us alone. Though dreadful situations may arise, we can depend on God's protective love to shield us, protect us, and deliver us.

Prayer of the Day:

"Lord, I thank you for love and protection. I offer up to you my fears and concerns this day. I trust that you will be with me and deliver me. Amen"

Charge of the Day:

Write down one memory where you were protected by God's unfailing love and concern.

Thought of the Day:

A picture is worth a thousand words and a memory can contain a life story.

Day 5

Moving the Heavens

God moves on David's behalf

In recent times, though the quest for spirituality has increased, the belief in the only living God stands in controversy. Some believe that some impersonal force caused all things and we are left to work life out on our own. This is simply not true.

We must stand in faith believing and knowing that God is not impersonal. He is not a corporation or faceless religious conglomerate. He remains actively involved in the world events and in the affairs of men.

He bowed the heavens also, and came

down: and darkness was under his feet. Psalms 18:9 (KJV)

David realized that in the midst of his troubles, God responded to him personally. He states that God bowed the heavens. This reveals God's personal intervention on his behalf. He also writes that darkness was under his feet. This shows us that God will rule in our darkest situations; He has mastery and control.

For those who are experiencing perplexing circumstances, realize that God is concerned and will personally intervene. Don't lose faith because the situation arises, knowing that He will be faithful to you to bring you through.

Prayer of the Day:

"Lord, help me to trust your love and concern. I thank you that you are personally concerned and involved with the events of my life.

Amen."

Charge of the Day:

Take inventory of your walk with God. Write down three times where the Lord demonstrated His personal intervention in your life.

Thought of the Day:

As the earth revolves around the sun, let your life revolve around the reality of God.

Day 6

Angels to the Rescue

God sends His angel

From man's most ancient times, the belief in supernatural beings involved in world events has existed. The Bible is replete with accounts of supernatural agents of God known as angels. Both Testaments establish that angels do exist.

Though God utilizes angels, they are not to be worshipped, venerated, or sought out for revelation or information. Angels are sent by the will of God to intervene on our behalf (*Therefore, angels are only servants--spirits sent to care for people who will inherit salvation – Hebrews 1:14 NLT*).

Some Christians believe that God no longer uses angels for believers, however, the scriptures give no indication this. Angels were active even after Jesus' resurrection, and seen by Peter, John, and Paul.

And he rode upon a cherub, and did fly: yea, he did fly upon the wings of the wind. He made darkness his secret place; his pavilion round about him were dark waters and thick clouds of the skies. At the brightness that was before him his thick clouds passed, hail stones and coals of fire.
Psalms 18:10-12 (KJV)

David realized that God's personal intervention was accomplished using angels. He recognized that His angel was the agent of deliverance.

What situations are confronting you? You can be assured that God's angels are with you.

There are numerous Christians which attest to this fact. Trust that God's presence is not only with you, but in times of great need the angels will be there to also protect.

Prayer of the Day:

"Lord, I thank you for your presence. I thank you that you also gave angels to help us in this life as well. Amen."

Charge of the Day:

Think of a time when you believed that an angel was involved in an event of your life.

Thought of the Day:

I would rather walk on the water with Christ rather than stay in the ship without Him.

Day 7

Victorious Voice

His voice still Thunders

Growing up, I became acquainted with the slogan, "When E. F. Hutton talks, people listen." This was a major marketing slogan for that firm. It gave the impression that what was said was not only important but could make impressive changes in one's life if followed.

Have you ever known someone whose word carried great weight and force? When they speak or give counsel, you just know that it is beneficial.

The LORD also thundered in the heavens, and the Highest gave his voice; hail stones and coals of fire. Yea, he sent out his

arrows, and scattered them; and he shot out lightnings, and discomfited them. Psalms 18:13-14 (KJV)

David recognized that his victory and deliverance were caused by the determination of the Father. He realized that it was at God's word that the victory that he experienced was possible.

On this day, realize that with a word, God can changed the detrimental events of life. When the disciples were in the storm at sea, Jesus stood up and spoke a word. Trust that God still speaks and His voice still thunders causing change.

Do not lose faith and hope. God will speak to you, for you, and on your behalf bring peace, comfort, and joy.

Prayer of the Day:

"I trust you on this day Lord that your voice still thunders and your word will stand in my life. I stand in faith on your love and grace. Thank you for all things. Amen."

Charge of the Day:

Recall situations that God intervened on your behalf. Make an effort to tell someone about one of them.

Thought of the Day:

Man creates problems, but God creates solutions.

Day 8

He Controls the Seas

God can calm the storms of life

Weather conditions usually dictate our daily activities. Those familiar with boating understand that the wrong weather can make for a harrowing adventure at sea. Life can be as a journey at sea. We constantly have to navigate the different "weather patterns" as we live daily.

In Both Testaments, we see God's power over the natural seas and waters. In Creation, He separated the waters into seas, lakes, and atmosphere. He divided the Red Sea. He caused the waters of Jordan to part in two. Jesus calmed the sea when the disciples were in the storm.

Then the channels of waters were seen, and the foundations of the world were discovered at thy rebuke, O Lord, at the blast of the breath of thy nostrils. He sent from above, he took me, he drew me out of many waters. Psalms 18:15-16 (KJV)

David likened his situation as tumultuous waters as seen in a storm. However, as God rebuked the waters to let dry land surface in Creation, so God delivered David from his calamities.

We can sometimes feel like we are a ship lost at sea during a storm. God power extends from natural phenomenon to the stormy occurrences in the lives of men. On today, realize that God has the power to bring peace to every storm in your life. Do not lose faith.

Prayer of the Day:

"I come before you on today Lord asking for grace to trust you during the stormy times of life. I thank you now. Amen."

Charge of the Day:

Do something that you have put off doing in your life that will enhance your relationship with Christ.

Thought of the Day:

The one who knows to do good and fails to do so, is the one who fails himself.

Day 9

Escaping My Enemies

David is delivered from his enemies

The world is fueled by relationships. They form the basis of existence. However, not all relationship are good. Some relationships are based upon mutual dislike, distrust, and sometimes hatred. People become enemies. Sometimes the feeling is mutual and at other times one-sided.

The Christian must recognize that we cannot hold bitterness and hatred toward anyone, even when we are wronged. Even when someone accounts us as an enemy, we must maintain forgiveness and demonstrate love. In doing so, God will be the one to deal with those who trouble us because He is the righteous judge.

> *He delivered me from my strong enemy, and from them which hated me: for they were too strong for me. They prevented me in the day of my calamity: but the LORD was my stay. Psalms 18:17-18 (KJV)*

God will always look out for us. Hence, He does not want us to take matters into our own hands when people are deliberately hurtful and malicious. He does not want us to be bound by bitterness, anger, and hatred.

David experienced God's deliverance from those who sought to kill him. He did not have to face them or deal with them in his own power and strength. We can learn from this.

Enemies will surface from in and outside of the Church. But, we can leave the dispensing of justice to God who holds the souls of men in mind. Do not avenge yourself, remember vengeance belongs to God (Romans 12:19).

Prayer of the Day:

I ask for help on today. I need grace to deal with those that count me an enemy. Help me to demonstrate your love and peace. Amen."

Charge of the Day:

Take self-inventory on today. Reflect on your growth or decline. Respond to God in prayer.

Thought of the Day:

You prove how much you know, when you recognize what you do not know.

Day 10

Make Room for Me

David is set in a Large Place

The story of there being no room at the inn is portrayed yearly in Christmas plays and productions. Mary and Joseph had to return Judah for the regional census. Seeing that it was mandated by the government, individuals converged on the cities of Jerusalem, resulting in the local inns being filled to capacity. Mary was full term and went into labor. OF course, the story ends in Jesus having to be born along side animals and placed in a manger.

What is significant about this. Some of you reading may feel like you have purpose and plans for your life, but there is no room for promotion on your job or even room for your ministry in the Church. However, Mary was able to being forth Jesus in an unexpected place. Hence, room was made for delivery in an unlikely place. However, Mary and Jesus survived, ultimately leading to the salvation of the world.

> ***He brought me forth also into a large place; he delivered me, because he delighted in me. Psalms 18:19 (KJV)***

In today's verse, we find David in a similar situation. David recalled how on many occasions he was boxed in. He was destined to be king and had years of fleeing from Saul. However, God eventually gave him victory and made room for him to sit on the throne.

From both these accounts, we discover that God will bring purpose forward in your life even when it seems like there is no room for it or no way for it to be achieved. Christ came forth in unusual circumstances and David became king against all odd. On today, know that God with you and will bring forth His purpose in your life.

Prayer of the Day:

"Lord, help me to maintain faith against the odds. I trust that Your will for my life will prosper. Amen."

Charge of the Day:

Encourage someone in their walk with the Lord.

Thought of the Day:

Almost every birth comes through pain. Pain and pressures are a part of achieving purpose.

Day 11

Keep It Holy

God is our Example of Holiness

Man, oh Man! Nowadays right is being called wrong and wrong is being justified (and being called right), even in the Church. Today, let us never lose sight of the fact that God is holy and desires holiness from those who serve Him.

We are free in Christ, but we are not free to do and say what we want to do. Holiness is just not a catch phrase, but it is to be a standard of morality and living; for all who are in Christ (regardless of denomination). Peter said it like this,

But as he which hath called you is holy, so

be ye holy in all manner of conversation; Because it is written, Be ye holy; for I am holy. 1 Peter 1:15-16 (KJV)

Jesus is holy and we should reflect His holiness. We cannot use our humanity as an excuse not to live a life that is pleasing to Him. God makes such a demand because He will give us all the help and support, we need in order to please Him.

Self-control and discipline can prove to be difficult, but not impossible. He did call us to Himself for us to fail. Realize on today, through faith and patience, you can walk in holiness. Again, keep it holy!

Prayer of the Day:

"I know that I can trust you God but help me to reflect your holiness daily. I thank you that you will never leave me and will help me. Amen."

Charge of the Day:

Consider on today: "Will individuals recognize that God is holy by my lifestyle?"

Thought of the Day:

I would rather be holy and rejected of men, rather than accepted of men and rejected by God.

Day 12

If You Are Wondering

He will do what is Best for You

Life is filled with numerous uncertainties. We do not always know what will happen in our lives. Though this is true, believers should not walk around in doubt and fear. Once we have received Christ, we can trust that He will be with us at all times.

There is never a time when He is not present. He is there; He cares and offers help. Today, remind yourself of His presence in your life. The enemy will cause you to doubt the one assurance that He gave us when He said that He would never leave us nor forsake us.

Let your conversation be without covetousness; and be content with such

things as ye have: for he hath said, I will never leave thee, nor forsake thee. Heb 13:5 (KJV)

So, if you are wondering how the situation is going to turn out: Stop and know He will do what is best for you. If you are wondering if He is going to answer that prayer: Stop and know that His ears are open to the cries of His people.

If you are wondering if He sees and knows what you are going through: Stop and know that His eyes are upon the righteous.

Just in case you are wondering if He is there or if He cares or if He will forgive, remember that He is God and He does not change. Do not think you can make God change His mind concerning you because His thoughts toward you are for good and He will bring forth good, and even the best in every situation.

Prayer of the Day:

"I trust you on this day Lord that you will intervene on my behalf. I stand in faith on your love and grace. Thank you for all things. Amen."

Charge of the Day:

Recall situations that God intervened on your behalf. Make an effort to tell someone about one of them.

Thought of the Day:

You don't need to know the answers to your problems, only the One who can solve all problems.

Day 13

I Just Don't Know!
Keep Your Eyes Toward the Lord

Knowledge is very important to the human existence. Knowledge fortified with understanding is crucial. Hence, the bible states that in "all thy getting, get an understanding." However, in life, there are times when we just do not know. Consequently, this leaves many not knowing what to do either.

Have you ever been (or are you now) in a place where you do not know what to do? We are instructed as Christians to pursue God and to walk with Him. Yet, there are circumstances and situations that come into our lives that leave us baffled. This is what Jehoshaphat experienced.

O our God, wilt thou not judge them? for we have no might against this great company that cometh against us; neither know we what to do: but our eyes are upon thee. 2 Chron 20:12 (KJV)

You do not know if you are praying correctly. You do not know what actions to take. You do not know if the situation that you are in could have been avoided. If it could have, then you are left not knowing what God will do.

On today, I want to encourage you that regardless of your present situations, trust God. Even in the midst of not knowing what do, trust and have faith that God will ensure that what is best for you will be manifested.

Remember His love, grace, mercy, and peace never fail. God will never forsake His people, nor leave us to fend for ourselves, even when we may have been at fault. If your cry today is, "I Just Don't Know!"

Understand that God knows all things and will be faithful to see you through. Though you may not know what to do with your situation, you can know what to do in the midst of it – TRUST GOD!

Prayer of the Day:

"I come before you on today Lord asking for grace to do what I know to do is right. Help me to have the proper response to the situations that are in my life. I thank you now. Amen."

Charge of the Day:

Throughout the day, thank God for the direction and provision He will give you.

Thought of the Day:

Knowledge is power and the knowledge of God is wisdom.

Day 14

The Reason for the Season

Understanding God's Purposes

God is a God of purpose. Regardless of the events that take place in our lives, there is a purpose. We do not serve a God who is clueless or useless. He is an omnipotent and all things occur by His will. Because of this, there is a reason for this season in your life.

> *To everything there is a season, and a time to every purpose under the heaven: A time to be born, and a time to die; a time to plant, and a time to pluck up that which is planted; A time to kill, and a time to heal; a time to break down, and a time to build*

up. *Eccl 3:1-3 (KJV)*

Just as there are necessary changes for natural seasons, there are spiritual seasons that all must pass through. Whether you are in a season of peace or war, riches or poverty, sickness or health, His plan for your life is unfolding. Seek God and He will reveal to you by His Spirit, the reason for this season.

Prayer of the Day:

I ask you on today for wisdom for my life. Help to understand the season that I am in at this time in my walk with you. Amen."

Charge of the Day:

Take self-inventory on today. Reflect on your growth or decline. Respond to God in prayer.

Thought of the Day:

Life brings changes, but a life in God brings

necessary changes for growth and success.

Day 15

Blessed Assurance
Thank God for Eternal Life

As a young boy, one of my favorite hymns was "Blessed Assurance." Though I had no personal relationship with the Lord, the words seemed so powerful and assuring. But today, I can appreciate the words of this song and it is still a favorite.

To know that I have a relationship with God through Christ gives me such hope and peace in a world filled with toils and trials.

Having predestinated us unto the adoption of children by Jesus Christ to himself, according to the good pleasure of his will, To the praise of the glory of his grace,

wherein he hath made us accepted in the beloved. In whom we have redemption through his blood, the forgiveness of sins, according to the riches of his grace. Eph 1:5-7 (KJV)

On today, remember that Jesus is with you. He will never leave you or forsake you. His daily presence in our lives keeps and strengthens us. It also reassures us of the hope of eternal life. There is a day coming where we will enter into our rest for eternity. This is the heart of the Christian's "Blessed Assurance."

Prayer of the Day:

"Lord, I thank you for the assurance of salvation and eternal life. I will praise you and give you thanks for it. Amen."

Charge of the Day:

Forgive someone on today who, directly or

indirectly, has offended you. Remember that God through Christ forgave you for all over your sins.

Thought of the Day:

The Message of Salvation: a gift that should always be re-gifted.

Day 16

I Can't Go Back
Standing in the Faith

Life is filled with many obstacles. This is just a proven fact. Aside from the difficulties that life can bring, maintaining a vibrant, walk with Christ can seem more like a burden than a blessing.

If we are brutally honest with ourselves, we can attest to feeling like it had been better not to have known Christ because knowledge of Him brings responsibilities with never ending spiritual warfare. However, in light of these things, we still have to have as our statement of faith, "I Can't Go Back!"

And Jesus said unto him, No man, having put his hand to the plough, and looking

back, is fit for the kingdom of God. Luke 9:62 (KJV)

Though times can get hard, people can misunderstand you, and God can seem unresponsive to you, going back to world and its lusts is simply not an option. Remember, salvation has promise in the life to come and also in this one. We have to take Peter's stance when Christ asked them would they leave Him also. Peter said where can we go, you have the words of eternal life.

In Christ, there is life and if we do not ever get what we want in this life, in the life to come there is everlasting joy, peace, and health. This is the HOPE of our salvation.

Prayer of the Day:

"I know that I can trust you God, you know what is right and wrong. Help me to do what is necessary to please you and move forward in the faith. Amen."

Charge of the Day:

Spend some time in prayerful meditation. Ask God to show you areas of sin in your life.

Thought of the Day:

The problem may be sin, but the solution is Christ.

Day 17

Anyway You Bless Me

Contentment in God's Will

We hear this saying in testimonies and in songs, "Any way You bless me, I'll be satisfied!" Some of us may have even used it ourselves. Yet, do we really mean it? If God chooses to bless us in a manner that we did not think of, we will be satisfied with His choice, or will we be still be unappreciative?

The scriptures tell us that God satisfies the mouth with good things. This shows us that whatever things we could ask or desire, He will perform it. However, we must trust that He gives to us in accordance to His will.

O satisfy us early with thy mercy; that we may rejoice and be glad all our days. Psalms 90:14-15 (KJV)

Some of you reading this are frustrated because it seems as if God has not given you specifically what you asked for. It does not mean He does not give us what we ask for, but He loves you enough to give you that which will satisfy you.

Food can only do you good if it is eaten and digested. The same is true with receiving from God. If you trust His wisdom and receive whatever He gives to you, you will find satisfaction and renewal as the scriptures state. So, the next time you say, "Any8way You Bless Me," make sure you mean it. Cause if you do, you will find yourself walking in greater peace, satisfaction, and renewed strength in Him.

Prayer of the Day:

"I trust you on this day Lord. You will provide some cool refreshing in the midst of the heat of life. I thank you for it now. Amen."

Charge of the Day:

Take some time to praise God in worship, rather than complain about present conditions.

Thought of the Day:

A Christian without faith is like a pool without water.

Day 18

Don't Give Up
It is Not Time to Quit

Have you ever thought about giving up? Life can come at you fast and spiritual warfare can seem endless. Sometimes, you may just want to throw in the towel. This is not just talking about giving up on one's salvation, but on your hopes, dreams, ambitions, and the promise of God.

Paul, like many of us, experienced many difficult circumstances and situations. However, he acknowledged the difficulties, but reveals the secret to his success. He allowed his inner man to remain strengthened by the Spirit of the Lord; though troubles, trials, and tests surrounded him.

> ***For which cause we faint not; but though our outward man perish, yet the inward man is renewed day by day. For our light affliction, which is but for a moment, worketh for us a far more exceeding and eternal weight of glory. 2 Cor 4:16-17 (KJV)***

So, for those who are tired and think that nothing is going to change – DON'T GIVE UP. Do not give up on God, His Word, His Promises, or His Church. Allow God to strengthen you in your spirit. Remember, in order to get through, you have to go through. Continue to be steadfast, unmovable, always abounding in His work. It is not in vain.

Prayer of the Day:

"I thank you for your willingness to give me strength and grace to stand. I give you thanks for it on today. Amen."

Charge of the Day:

Take some time on today and thank God for the abundance of His grace and mercy.

Thought of the Day:

Forgive others as God through Christ has forgiven you.

Day 19

All Things are Possible
Only Believe

It is common for those who have an inkling of faith in God to say that He can do anything. This sentiment is echoed in sermons, songs, and sayings in the Christian community.

He consistently proves Himself in His works in our lives. However, our declaration of God's ability in making the impossible very much possibly goes beyond His mighty acts.

> *Behold, I am the LORD, the God of all flesh: is there anything too hard for me? Jer 32:27 (KJV)*

God's salvation through Christ also saves us from ourselves. The ability of God to transform the heart of an individual born in sin is the greatest demonstration of His power. Through the work of the Holy Spirit, we can be partakers of the impossible. We can be saved and transformed into the image of Christ and live a life that is pleasing to Him.

Regardless of your quirks, hang-ups, faults, weakness, dispositions, and mind-sets, God can and will deliver. With Him, all things are possible.

Prayer of the Day:

Lord, give me grace, peace, and strength to have the faith comparable to your awesome power. I will trust in your ability to increase my faith. Amen."

Charge of the Day:

Remember times when you thought God had

forsaken you, but in the end proved to be faithful.

Thought of the Day:

Whatever God promises, He is more than able to perform.

Day 20

In His Name

Remembering the Authority of His Name

What's in a name? Why is it so important that all things are given a name? The number one reason is that a name brings identity to an object. For the believer, Jesus is the name that gives us identity.

It is in this name that we are saved, healed, and delivered. However, there are situations that come wherein we sometimes forget to call upon that name.

That at the name of Jesus every knee should bow, of things in heaven, and things in earth, and things under the earth; And that every tongue should confess that Jesus Christ is Lord, to the glory of God the Father. Phil 2:10-11 (KJV)

At the mention of His name, demons tremble and bodies are healed. In the midst of your trials and tests, do not forget to SAY the name, BELIEVE the name, and TRUST the name.

For the name of Jesus is a strong tower and defense in the life of the Christian – Proverbs 18:10 (KJV). Regardless of what is presently in your life, the mention of His name will open up the path to freedom and deliverance.

Prayer of the Day:

"Lord, grant me grace to trust that you will renew, revive, and restore things in my life that have been lost by the power and authority of Christ's name. I thank you for what you will do. Amen."

Charge of the Day:

Ask God to come into situations where you have suffered and felt loss, expecting restoration.

Thought of the Day:

God is compassionate and remembers times of heartache and pain in our lives.

Day 21

Walking Upright
Abraham Hears from God

Salvation through Jesus Christ is a great and precious gift. Though it is free, there is a cost involved. As recipients of God's grace, He requires those that come to Him to live in accordance to His standards. Some view this as legalism or a burden; however, the scriptures are clear that God's expects His followers to walk upright.

Abraham received a great promise from God. He experienced God's personal intervention in his life. However, God appeared to Abraham, challenging his lifestyle and conduct as a servant of God.

> *And when Abram was ninety years old and nine, the Lord appeared to Abram, and*

said unto him, I am the Almighty God; walk before me, and be thou perfect. And I will make my covenant between me and thee, and will multiply thee exceedingly. Gen 17:1-2 (KJV)

God appears to Abraham and charges him to walk before Him and be perfect; that is, mature. As Christians, we cannot forget that we have to do that which is right.

Though some challenge this by stating that God is merciful and loving; it is understood that His mercy and love is there to help us as we strive to overcome the lust of the eyes, the lusts of the flesh, and the pride of life.

His righteous standards are given to us by His discretion and with His assistance. On today, examine aspects of your life. Be honest with God and with yourself. Make a new commitment to walking upright before Him.

Prayer of the Day:

"Lord, I thank you for your mercy, goodness, kindness, and grace. On today, I commit myself to doing that which pleases you in my daily life. I am grateful for your help and strength to overcome external and internal challenges. Amen."

Charge of the Day:

Take some time today for self-evaluation. Recognize your strengths and weakness and present them to God in prayer.

Thought of the Day:

God wants you to overcome. If you want to overcome and He wants you to overcome, then nothing can stop you from overcoming.

~

Day 22

Humble Yourself
Abraham bows before God

Do you know someone who is arrogant and proud? Have seen individuals who are servants of Christ who do not walk in humility? They are not humble before men and even God. Never use your personal relationship with Christ as an excuse to disobey and rebel when it suits you. God resists those who are proud, but those who are humble can expect to receive an infinite supply of His grace.

Though Abraham received the covenant promises of God, he continually humbled himself. After God commanded him to walk upright before Him, Abraham humbles himself and bows before the Lord.

And Abram fell on his face: and God talked with him, saying, As for me, behold, my covenant is with thee, and thou shalt be a father of many nations. Gen 17:3-4 (KJV)

How do you respond to God's word whether by inspiration, revelation, or a sermon? When you hear or read it, do you humble yourself before God? Or, do you justify how you are rather than allow His words to be the governing factor in your life?

Abraham humbled himself and God, once again, established His covenant with him. His humility set him up for a blessing. When we humble ourselves before the Lord, we set the stage for God to do great things that He has purposed for us. On today, take time to examine your humility level before God. If it is low, adjust it and see how it will change your life.

Prayer of the Day:

"I thank you that you abide with those who are humble. On this day, I humble myself before you, acknowledging your awesome power, but gentle grace. I thank you for all you are to me. Amen"

Charge of the Day:

List three areas of your life where you could use a little more humility and grace.

Thought of the Day:

Humility is the key to promotion, while pride will demote you and destroy you.

~

Day 23

Changing Self-Perceptions

Abraham Receives a Name Change

Many people do not have the proper perception of themselves. Because of this, many Christians do not know how to view themselves even as recipients of God's salvation. They struggle with who they were, who they are, and who they will become. Our relationship with Christ brings us into a new life with a new identity. The Christian, thus, has to see himself as God sees him and receive his new identity in Christ.

Neither shall thy name any more be called Abram, but thy name shall be Abraham; for a father of many nations have I made

thee. And I will make thee exceeding fruitful, and I will make nations of thee, and kings shall come out of thee. Gen 17:5-6 (KJV)

Abraham received the promise of a son, but that was not enough from God's viewpoint. His coming blessing required that Abraham no longer view himself in the same manner. God changes his name from Abram (which means Exalted Father) to Abraham (Father of Many). God changed His name while he was only the father of one; that is Ishmael. Abraham's name change signified what God had purposed him to be. However, his name signified his relationship and covenant with God.

The Christian today has to receive a spiritual name change. Though people may call you by the same name, it should not have the same impact.

However, it will begin with you agreeing with God and with who you are in Him.

On today, if you know that you do not see yourself, as God would have you, ask for grace and strength. He will help you develop the proper self-perception. You will not think too high of yourself or too low of yourself. Remember, if any man is in Christ, he is a new creation.

Prayer of the Day:

"I thank you that who I was before you does not characterize who I am now in you. I ask you to help me to see myself as you see me. I desire to have the proper self-perception. Amen."

Charge of the Day:

Consider these three things: "How do I think others view me?" – "How do I view myself?" – How do I think God sees me?": Do they agree or differ?

Thought of the Day:

I want others to accept me and love me; but if not, I will settle for the fact that God sees me totally for who I am and loves me anyway.

Day 24

Cutting Away

Abraham Commanded to Circumcise

Jesus' teachings challenged the very sensibilities of His listeners. On one occasion, He tells them that if a part of their body offended them, they were to cut it off. Though symbolic in nature, the sentiment is evident; the Christian should be willing to get rid of anything that would hinder their walk with Christ. Abraham faced a similar challenge.

God established His promises and covenants with him; however, to show his agreement and submission to what God had promised, he had to circumcise himself and his household.

And ye shall circumcise the flesh of your foreskin; and it shall be a token of the covenant betwixt me and you. Gen 17:11 (KJV)

It can be difficult to get rid of things in our lives that are dear and personal. Abraham had to experience physical pain in demonstration of his faithfulness to God. In addition, the males that were under his care would suffer the same pain.

Likewise, when the Christian decides to cut away people, places, and things from his or her life, it may cause pain. Yet, the Christian must know that it will be worth it, in this life and in the life to come.

Today, what people, places, and things are in your life that need to be cut away so that you can be fruitful in your walk with Christ? Are you willing to face the pains of self-denial and separation from others?

Just know that God will give grace, peace, and strength to those who will sacrifice themselves for Him. Make a decision today that you will cut away those things that will prevent you from progressing in Christ.

Prayer of the Day:

"Lord, I need your help to cut away things that will frustrate my walk with you. I thank you for the grace, peace, and strength to do it. Amen"

Charge of the Day:

Recognize people, places, and things that need to be cut away for personal growth.

Thought of the Day:

I would rather go to heaven with nothing that into hell with everything.

Day 25

Seeing Others as God's Does

God Changes Sarai's Name

In life, we will encounter many people with varying personalities and dispositions. It is a fact that there will be disagreements, fallouts, and times of miscommunication. These things can cause an individual not to have the proper perspective of others in daily interactions. It can be difficult to see others, especially as God sees them, when we have seen unfavorable aspects of their personalities and lifestyles.

> *And God said unto Abraham, As for Sarai thy wife, thou shalt not call her name Sarai, but Sarah shall her name be. Gen 17:15 (KJV)*

Abraham receives a name change, but God goes further and changes the name of his wife. Abraham had to see his wife, no longer as a barren woman (Sarai), but as a fruitful woman from whom kings and nations would come (Sarah).

Once we come to Christ, our perception of men has to change. We have to see others as God does. He is not willing that any should perish. The very worst of sinners are candidates for His grace and redemption. When we see others as God does, it will restrain us from allowing what we see and know about them to change our love for them. This holds especially true concerning other members of the Body of Christ.

Though some Christians may be like Sarai, being barren in their walks with Christ, we must see them as candidates for being Sarah, members who will eventually be of great service to the

Church and Kingdom of God. This will keep us from unforgiveness, bitterness, and judgment.

Prayer of the Day:

"Lord, help me to get over what I know about others. Help me to get past what has offended me to see them as you do. I thank you for it. Amen."

Charge of the Day:

Make an effort to invite God's presence into places of offense caused through others. Allow His grace to bring you into a place of love and forgiveness.

Thought of the Day:

The golden rule is still a good rule to adopt.

Day 26

Letting Go

Abraham pleads for Ishmael

Friends, family, and acquaintances are important to our lives. We live in a world where we must interact and be interdependent upon others for love, support, and relationship. However, some individuals in our lives may prove to be useful only at certain times in our lives. It does not mean that there is a problem; however, God may want to bring others into our lives for continual growth and success in Him.

Abraham had to learn the reality of this truth. Because God's promise was upon Sarah and Isaac, he would eventually have to let go of Ishmael that God's promises to him would be established. However, Abraham protested.

> **And Abraham said unto God, O that Ishmael might live before thee! Gen 17:18 (KJV)**

Abraham loved Ishmael, but God's covenant would be with Isaac. Abraham pleaded with God for Ishmael. On today, what people are in your life that you know that they will not be able to be with you always? Are you willing to let them go {not because you hate them or any problem exists} for the sake of continual growth and success in Christ?

They may be longtime friends and family members. It does not mean that there is no communication and fellowship, but their influence in your life has to be limited that God may bring to you all that He has for you. This may be a difficult task, but in the end, everyone will prosper. Later on, in this story, we discover that God blessed Ishmael, though he had to leave his father.

Prayer of the Day:

"I know that I can trust you God, you know what is best for me and who is good for me. Help me to do what is necessary to please you. Amen."

Charge of the Day:

Spend some time in prayerful meditation. Ask God to show you individuals that you may need to let go of.

Thought of the Day:

Being alone is not the same as being lonely.

Day 27

Deliver Me from Me

Facing the enemy of self

It is interesting to note that much external opposition exists to frustrate our walk and growth in Christ. However, there is an enemy that we must all face; that is, the enemy of self. We may be able to escape people, circumstances, and situations, but where can you run from yourself. Every Christian has to come to a place where they ask God to deliver them from themselves.

> *Keep back thy servant also from presumptuous sins; let them not have dominion over me: then shall I be upright, and I shall be innocent from the great transgression. Psalms 19:13 (KJV)*

David prayed that God would keep him from personal sins and weaknesses; that the things that he may want to do would not have dominion over him. This is to be our prayer. Once we have received forgiveness and freedom in Christ, we are not to allow the desires of the flesh to rule us.

When we ask God to deliver us from ourselves, we set ourselves us for victory in every area of our lives. Let your prayer be this day, "Deliver Me from Me."

Prayer of the Day:

"I thank you for the truth that your power to deliver extends to my internal struggles with self. I praise you for present and future freedom. Amen."

Charge of the Day:

Take some time on today and relax.

Thought of the Day:

I have to live with myself so I need to become a better roommate.

Day 28

A Qualified Christian

The Christian Example

It should be the desire of every Christian to be a useful and productive servant of the Lord; that is, a worthy Christian. On any job, qualified individuals are sought to fill positions. We know that anyone that is qualified makes necessary adjustments and work hard to obtain the necessary skills.

The same is true of the Christian. We have to be willing to adjust and work towards being a qualified and productive servant. Jesus' words to the disciples reveal to us that He would have it no other way.

Ye are the salt of the earth: but if the salt have lost his savour, wherewith shall it be salted? it is thenceforth good for nothing, but to be cast out, and to be trodden under foot of men. Matt 5:13 (KJV)

The qualified Christian's standard for thought, doctrine, and practice is the Word of God. The qualified Christian knows that life has to be governed by the eternal Word of God. Let this be your desire, hope, and plea that you will become and remain a qualified Christian.

Prayer of the Day:

"Lord, give me grace, peace, and strength to become a qualified Christian.

Amen."

Charge of the Day:

Exercise patience in a situation that would normally irritate and upset you.

Thought of the Day:

Acceptance of personal weakness is a sign of great strength.

Day 29

I Am Stuck

Overcoming Complacency

Have you ever felt like this? Though life progresses on, sometimes we can get in a place where there is no movement or transition. You can be busy as ever and still stuck in the same place. However, there is hope, especially for the Christian.

> *The impotent man answered him, Sir, I have no man, when the water is troubled, to put me into the pool: but while I am coming, another steppeth down before me. John 5:7 (KJV)*

In the scriptures, we read of an impotent

man who wanted to be healed but, in essence, he was stuck. Has it ever seemed that everyone seems to be progressing in life, ministry, etc, while your efforts at success are frustrated? Then, you can identify with the plight of this man. He witnessed others get healed for years while he remained sick. Yet, that was not the end of his story.

When Jesus appeared, He offered and gave the man the deliverance that he had desired for years. The same applies to you today. Regardless of how long you may have been "stuck," Jesus is still able to bring you into another place in your life. Reach out to Him again in faith and prayer knowing that your cry will no longer be, "I Am Stuck."

Prayer of the Day:

"Lord, grant me grace to move forward from areas of struggle. I thank you now for it. Amen."

Charge of the Day:

Write a letter to God describing how you feel about what you are going through.

Thought of the Day:

The blessings of the Lord upon you are for you and those associated with you.

Day 30

I Am Tired

Dealing with Spiritual Exhaustion

I am tired. There is so much to do and so little time to do it. Is this how you feel? Even in your relationship with God, trying to progress can seem to become difficult. However, to escape the tiredness and weariness that comes with life, one must look to Christ.

> ***And let us not be weary in well doing: for in due season we shall reap, if we faint not. Gal 6:9 (KJV)***

Paul admonished the Galatians not to allow weariness to overtake them. Oftentimes one becomes tired and weary where there is no goal or prize in front of them. However, the Christian knows that God will remember all of his labors and toils; especially those endeavors we do in His name. We can become tired physically, but when a person becomes spiritually exhausted, the effects can be devastating on a person's outlook and experience. Yet, trust God will take note and give you rest.

On this day, ask the Lord to give you peace, strength, and hope that can only come from Him. Your cry, then, will no longer be, "I Am Tired!"

Prayer of the Day:

"Lord, I thank you for your mercy, goodness, kindness, and grace. On today, I commit myself to receiving peace and inner rest from you. Amen."

Charge of the Day:

Take some time today for self-evaluation. Recognize your strengths and weakness and present them to God in prayer.

Thought of the Day:

God wants you to overcome. If you want to overcome and He wants you to overcome, then nothing can stop you from overcoming.

www.ingramcontent.com/pod-product-compliance
Lightning Source LLC
Chambersburg PA
CBHW050342010526
44119CB00049B/664